LifeCaps Presents:

Selfridge:

The Life and Times of Harry Gordon Selfridge

By Fergus Mason

BookCaps™ Study Guides

www.bookcaps.com

FERGUS MASON

Selfridge

Table of Contents

ABOUT LIFECAPS

LifeCaps is an imprint of BookCaps™ Study Guides. With each book, a lesser known or sometimes forgotten life is recapped. We publish a wide array of topics (from baseball and music to literature and philosophy), so check our growing catalogue regularly (www.bookcaps.com) to see our newest books.

INTRODUCTION

Just for a moment try to put every shopping trip you've ever made out of your head. Imagine a different world. Imagine that all the goods for sale are locked away in cabinets and to handle them, or even to examine them closely, you need to ask a shop assistant to open it up for you. Imagine that within seconds of entering a store a floorwalker approaches you and asks if you're planning to buy something – then, when you say "I'm just looking," rudely tells you to leave. Imagine any attempt to return faulty or unsuitable goods being met with ridicule, obstruction or a flat refusal to help you.

Until the late 19th century people didn't have to imagine that; it was reality. For anyone alive today a visit to the average store back then would convince you that they didn't really *want* to sell you anything. The idea of customer service was an alien one. Stores sold things. If you wanted to buy them, fine. If you didn't they weren't really interested. Browsing was strongly discouraged and impulse buys were almost unheard of. Shopping was something you did when you had to. It certainly wasn't something anyone enjoyed.

Then, in the late 1880s, one man came along and changed all that. He set out to make shopping fun, and to make the customer feel valued. He spread the idea that it was fine to just look around. He also introduced many of the concepts we now take for granted – the Christmas retail season, wedding gift lists, in-store entertainment and even the bargain basement. His name was Harry Gordon Selfridge.

Harry Selfridge grew up in small-town America after the Civil War, and tried his hand at a variety of careers before taking a job at one of Chicago's leading wholesalers. After a successful career in management he moved to the retail side of the business and instantly went to work on revolutionizing the way it worked.

What he'd accomplished by the age of fifty was more than enough to be proud of, but Selfridge wasn't content. Next he set himself the challenge of moving to London and founding a new, unique department store that would turn out be the prototype for every one that followed. That store is still in business more than a century later and it still bears his name.

For decades the name of Harry Selfridge has been almost forgotten, but a recent TV series from ITV and PBS has pushed his name back into the limelight. He's almost as well known today as he was on a wet March day in 1909 when his new store opened its doors to admit a flood of excited Londoners. TV drama is TV drama, though, and the story it tells is as manufactured as the image Selfridge created for himself so long ago. There's a lot more to it than what you can see on the screen – the struggle, the disappointments and above all the family who helped him on his way to success. *Mr. Selfridge* told the fairy tale version of the story; here's the real thing.

CHAPTER 1: THE YOUNG ENTREPRENEUR

Anyone who's ever moved to a new town knows what a challenge it can be. Starting off in an unfamiliar house, finding the best stores, getting to know new neighbors... it can be an intimidating prospect. So just imagine how it must have felt to the pioneers who moved west across America in the 19th century. They were heading into the unknown, not just moving to a new town but trying to establish one. To do that takes an incredible level of determination, which means it takes a special kind of person. Even when a settlement began to grow and take shape moving there was definitely not for the faint hearted. Many new towns grew fitfully for a few years then faded away; others prospered. It often took decades to be sure which way a town was going to go, so moving to a new settlement took real courage.

David P. Mapes had built a career hauling cut timber down the rivers of New York state on one of the new steam-powered riverboats. He was successful enough to get elected to the State Assembly in 1831, but it seems he wanted a bigger challenge. In 1845 he moved to Wisconsin, and sometime between then and 1846 he negotiated a land purchase from state land secretary John Scott Horner. It was an expensive undertaking because the purchase came with several conditions; within a year of taking over the land he had to build both a flour mill and an inn, and then run the inn himself for twelve months. In return he could use the water power from the mill's wheel for his own purposes, and would own every alternate lot in the new town. Horner also wanted the right to name the settlement, and as he was the one who controlled land allocation Mapes couldn't refuse. He did manage to impose some conditions of his own though; the name shouldn't be a personal one, it had to be unique in the USA, it wasn't to be a Native American name and it must be short. If the land secretary had any dreams of calling the town Hornerville they ended right there. Instead he settled on Ripon, after his English ancestors' hometown in Yorkshire.

In February 1849 Mapes moved to his new land with his two sons and their families, and began clearing the ground.[i] Within a year, as specified, the mill was running and the Ripon House Inn was open for business. Soon families started moving into the vacant plots and the town began to grow. It was an uphill struggle at first, because Ripon wasn't on a navigable river or close to the growing railway network, but it was surrounded by good prairie land and Mapes worked hard to attract settlers. On March 20, 1854 a new anti-slavery party was founded at a meeting in the Ripon schoolhouse and decided to call itself the Republican Party.[ii] In case that wasn't enough to bring in more people, Mapes gave away lots in the town on condition that the new owners made specified improvements to the land. Sometime in the early 1850s Robert and Lois Selfridge took up this offer and moved to Ripon. With them went their two children, Robert Jr. and Charles.

The couple's third son, Henry Gordon "Harry" Selfridge, was born in Ripon on January 11, 1856 (not 1858 as many people believe).[iii] Robert Oliver Selfridge was looking for an opportunity that would let him bring up his young family, and obviously he thought he could find it in this small new town in rural Wisconsin. Within months of Harry's birth, however, something new came along: he had the chance to buy the general store in Jackson, Michigan. Robert didn't hesitate; showing the same willingness to start again that had brought him to Ripon in the first place he uprooted his family again and moved 250 miles southeast to take over the store.

Five years later the store was a successful business, but now politics intervened. The Republican Party had come a long way from its first meeting in the Ripon schoolhouse, and by 1858 it was the dominant political force in most of the northern states. On November 6, 1860 the party's presidential candidate, Abraham Lincoln, won a four-way race to become the 16th President of the United States. The election triggered a rapid slide towards war.

The 1860 Republican platform had played down the slavery issue, causing outrage among the party's hardliners. Lincoln promised not to legislate against slavery in the states, but did hint at abolishing it in the territories. It was too moderate a position for many in his own party, but nowhere near moderate enough for the southern states where slavery was a major part of the agricultural industry. A group of state governors began planning secession and in February 1861 – just days before Lincoln was inaugurated as president on March 4 – seven states announced that they were leaving the USA to establish a confederacy. On April 12, Confederate forces attacked US forces in Fort Sumter, a fortress that controlled the entrance to Charleston Harbor, and Lincoln called for the states to provide 75,000 militia to suppress the Confederate Army. That request pushed four more states into joining the Confederacy and the war, limited up to that point, began to explode out of control. Within months, tens of thousands of men in both north and south had volunteered to join up and fight, and the Union Army started to swell from its peacetime strength of just 16,000 men towards a final total of over two million. One of those who volunteered was Robert Selfridge.

As far as the war itself went, Robert did fine; he became an officer in the Union Army and was eventually promoted to major. When the Confederacy surrendered in May 1865, he was demobilized along with hundreds of thousands more veterans, but while most of them returned home, Robert, for reasons unknown, decided not to. Instead he simply vanished, leaving no trace beyond a record of honorable discharge.[iv] Lois chose not to tell her sons what had happened; instead she told them that their father had been killed in action, a claim that Harry often repeated to newspapers through his life.[v] It was only much later that he learned the truth. Dead or vanished, however, Robert Selfridge was gone and either way the effect on Lois and her family was the same; she was left alone to bring up three young boys.

As much of a struggle as raising three children on her own must have been, it must still have been a shocking blow when Robert Jr. and Charles both died within a few months of the war's end. That left her with just Harry, but without her husband's army pay or the income from the now-sold general store she was still desperate for money. Finally she found a job as a schoolteacher, which gave her a small but regular income. At first she supplemented it by selling hand-painted greeting cards; eventually she worked her way up and became headmistress of the local high school.

In those early years after the war, it was a constant struggle to make ends meet, and at the age of ten Harry started to make his own contribution. He found work in the village store, delivering newspapers and collecting payments from customers; that brought in an extra $1.50 a week.[vi] Two years later he started working part-time at Leonard Field's dry goods store. When he was thirteen, he and a friend from school, Peter Loomis, began producing a monthly magazine for boys. Despite their age the two ran it as a proper business and even made money from selling advertising space. The experience gave young Harry a taste of life as an entrepreneur. It wasn't enough of an income, though, and soon he began looking for a full time job. Aged 14 he was offered a place as a clerk at a local bank, and left school to take it up – few states had compulsory schooling laws at the time and

Michigan wasn't among them, but even where school was mandatory the leaving age was 14.

Selfridge doesn't seem to have enjoyed the bank job very much – after the thrill of running his own small business with Loomis it's hard to blame him – but he had other plans. His ambition now was to become an officer in the US Navy, and that meant going through the United States Naval Academy at Annapolis. After four years at the Naval Academy successful midshipmen graduate with a degree and a commission, so competition has always been stiff. In the early 1870s it was even more so; the navy was being cut savagely in the aftermath of the Civil War and there were few vacancies for new officers. The Class of 1868 graduated only 25 officers and the total number of cadets at the time was less than 200. It took determination to get in, and physical standards were also high. Harry was charming and persuasive and probably had little trouble with the interview process, but when it came to his physical examination it was a different story. With so few vacancies, the Academy could afford to tighten its already strict standards, and there was no room for flexibility for those who didn't quite match up. One of those standards was a minimum height limit, and Harry Selfridge was just short of it – some sources say by only a quarter of an inch. That was enough for Annapolis to reject his application. It was a crushing disappointment for Selfridge, and left him with a lifelong sensitivity about his short stature.

After failing to get a place at Annapolis, Selfridge had to look for a new career. He initially returned to Jackson and found a job with a local furniture factory, working as a bookkeeper. Four months later, the company went out of business and Harry had to move on again. He found another bookkeeper's job, this time at an insurance office in Grand Rapids.

Selfridge's big break came in 1876 when Leonard Field, the owner of the dry goods store where he'd worked for a while, agreed to write him a letter of recommendation to Marshall Field. Marshall Field, who'd moved to Chicago from Massachusetts the year Harry was born, had worked for a Chicago dry goods chain for several years. Then in 1865 he and a colleague, Levi Leiter, bought out P. Palmer & Co., a rival store, and went into business for themselves. Three years later they moved the store into an impressive new building on State and Washington built by its original owner, Potter Palmer, who had moved into real estate. Field & Leiter, as it was called at the time, now sold a hugely expanded range of goods across six floors. Only three years later, the building was destroyed in the Great Chicago Fire of 1871, but the employees managed to save most of the merchandise before the building erupted into flames. Weeks later, Field & Leiter reopened in temporary premises, then moved back to State Street in 1873.

In 1876, when Selfridge applied for a job there, Marshall Field operated both the increasingly popular retail store and a much larger wholesale division. Selfridge was taken on in the stock department of the wholesale business, which supplied merchandise to many smaller stores throughout the Midwest and the western USA. As a junior stock boy his duties included breaking down bulk consignments of goods as they arrived at the warehouse and transferring them to the stock shelves from where the orders division would collect and ship them. It would have been hard work, hauling boxes around the huge building on a cart, and the turnover rate among employees was high. However, that meant there were opportunities for anyone who was prepared to stick with it. Harry Selfridge was prepared to stick with it, and he gradually advanced through the wholesale division.

Another fire destroyed the retail store in 1877, but by 1879 it was operating again in a new, even larger building on the State and Washington site. In 1881, Field bought out Leiter's share of the business and renamed the store Marshall Field & Co. It would remain as Chicago's leading department store until Macy's bought it out in 2006. Through this period the retail store continued to grow in importance. By 1887, while the wholesale side still brought in six times the income, the big store was the best known part of the business. That year the wholesale side of the company moved into a new seven-story Romanesque building that took up an entire block. It was much larger than the previous location and needed a bigger staff, so again there were promotion opportunities for the existing employees. Selfridge, by now a senior manager in the bulk stock department, was probably expecting another advancement. As it turned out he got it, but it moved him onto a new career path.

As the wholesale division moved into its new premises, Selfridge was told that instead of moving with it he was being transferred to the retail store as its new director – he would be in charge of that whole part of the business. It was a significant move, given that the share of Marshall Field's total profits generated by retail had been slowly rising for several years. Field himself clearly saw it as playing an even more important role in the future, and it says a lot for his opinion of Harry that he put him in charge of it at this point, when the wholesale store itself was going through a major expansion.

CHAPTER 2: REINVENTING RETAIL

When Harry Selfridge took over the retail arm of Marshall Field he was 31 years old and he'd been with the company for ten years. He'd worked his way up through what was still the more profitable side of the company and carried out a wide range of jobs, from his initial time as a stock boy to managing the flow of orders heading out to retailers across two-thirds of the USA. However, all his jobs with the company had been out of the public eye, and he hadn't been dealing face to face with customers.

Of course, as head of the entire store there was no real reason for him to deal with customers if he didn't want to. He had a general manager and a whole team of floor managers who could insulate him from the actual business of selling things to people. If he'd spent his days in his office, passing instructions down the chain and listening to the feedback that came back up it, nobody at Marshall Field would have thought any the worse of him. But that's not what he chose to do.

It looks as though moving to the retail side unlocked a buried potential in Harry. His only experience of facing customers directly had been long ago, as a boy working in the store back in Jackson. Now he had the opportunity to do it again, if he wanted, in a much grander setting. He threw himself into it enthusiastically. Instead of staying in his spacious office running the store remotely he spent every minute he could walking the sales floors, watching how his staff handled their jobs and – more importantly – watching the customers and how they spent their time inside the store.

Marshall Field had a lot in common with a modern department store in terms of its layout and what was available, but the way staff acted toward customers was very different – and in ways that wouldn't be anywhere close to acceptable today. Advertising standards were much looser and sellers could get away with what, now, would be seen as illegal misrepresentations. They often did get away with it, too. The law regarding sales in the USA was ruled by the principle of *caveat emptor* – "Let the buyer beware" – following an 1817 ruling by the Supreme Court in the *Laidlaw v. Organ* case. In 1815, Hector M. Organ had bought fifty tons of tobacco from trader Peter Laidlaw, and while they were drawing up the contract, Laidlaw asked Organ if he knew anything that might affect tobacco prices over the next few days. Organ said he didn't, but he was lying; his brother had told him that morning that the USA and Britain had just signed a treaty to end the War of 1812. During the war, the Royal Navy had blockaded the US coast, crippling trade and slashing the price of tobacco by half. Hours after Organ drove away with his wagonloads of tobacco, the news broke across the USA and the price soared. Laidlaw tried to get the goods back on the grounds that Organ had misled him, but first the District Court of Louisiana and then the US Supreme Court ruled that Organ had not been obliged to disclose relevant information.[vii] Although in this case it was the seller who had suffered (making it technically a case of *caveat venditor*), both retailers and wholesalers throughout the USA embraced the principle enthusiastically. About the only limit the courts placed on their actions was that sellers couldn't hide defects in their products, but they certainly didn't have to tell anyone about them. As the legal definition of "defect" included products that were completely unfit for their advertised purpose it was a minefield for shoppers, and they had very little chance of redress if they ended up being misled.

With such a free-for-all, and virtual immunity from legal action, it's perhaps natural that retail staff felt superior when dealing with customers and often let it show. If a customer did complain about a product or service they were usually fobbed off with excuses, with the *caveat emptor* argument available as an almost unbeatable weapon of last resort. It was what American shoppers were used to and, as Marshall Field's growing retail business showed, they mostly accepted it. Harry Selfridge watched and learned, and he soon decided that even if people were willing to put up with the retail industry the way it was, the store he was now running could – and should – do better.

What Selfridge set out to do was to fundamentally change the way retail staff and customers interacted. Instead of making people feel like they were barely tolerated in the store, a nuisance who disrupted the smooth running of the place, he told his staff to make them feel welcome. The first step was to revolutionize the way customer enquiries and complaints were handled. The service staff was ordered to stop trying to brush off customers who were unhappy with something they'd purchased; instead, their complaints were to be carefully and sympathetically listened to, and wherever possible, acted on. To help educate staff in what he expected of them, a new slogan was placed at the heart of the store's philosophy: "The customer is always right".

Of course the customer *isn't* always right; sometimes – often – they're spectacularly wrong, and anyone who works in retail has a store of funny stories about rude, mistaken or clueless customers.[viii] What Selfridge had realized, however, was that even when they are wrong it's usually just an honest misunderstanding, and that by treating them sympathetically staff could avoid arguments and ill feeling. If a customer tried to get a refund on a faulty product and was sent packing by a manager they would be resentful, and there was a good chance that next time they wanted something they'd go to a different store. On the other hand, if the staff were friendly and helpful it would leave people with a good impression of the store, and they'd be more likely to come back. After all, most complaints could be resolved without actually costing anything – refunding a sale usually meant the store got its goods back and could sell them again – and any losses that did occur would be offset by the higher chance of having that customer come back in the future.

History doesn't record whether the "customer is always right" slogan was coined by Selfridge or by Marshall Field himself, but it certainly fit with the ideas Selfridge was bringing to his new job. His aim was to make shopping at the store an enjoyable experience that people would feel enthusiastic about, and he was constantly trying out new tricks to make that happen. Other large stores, first in Chicago and then across the USA (an early one was the Philadelphia-based Wanamaker's) soon saw what was happening at Marshall Field and started to rejuvenate their own customer relations, but Selfridge was out in front of them and he had no intention of giving up his lead. The next innovation at Marshall Field was pure Selfridge, and it's still with us today.

For most retailers the weeks before Christmas are the most important part of the year. Today, department store takings in the USA are 50 per cent higher in December than in November. For other retail sectors the increase is even greater – 100 per cent in bookstores, 170 per cent for jewelers.[ix] In the 1880s the increase wasn't anywhere near as large as it is now, because gift-giving was a smaller part of the Christmas tradition, but it was still significant. Selfridge believed that by whipping up some enthusiasm among his customers he could boost sales; the question was how to do that. Most retailers didn't do much beyond getting in stocks of seasonal goods and putting up a few tired decorations, perhaps including the latest craze imported from Britain: a Christmas tree.

Anyone with a calendar could work out how many days remained until Christmas, but Selfridge decided to zero in on the days when they could visit his store. Sunday trading is now routine in most US states, although local "blue laws" might still impose restrictions, but that's not always been the case. In 1887, almost all stores were firmly closed on a Sunday, including Marshall Field. The same applied to public holidays like Thanksgiving. Selfridge figured out that by totaling up the number of days the store would be open he could generate the feeling of a countdown, reminding shoppers that their opportunities to buy Christmas gifts – plus decorations, food items and other seasonal items – were limited and steadily ticking away. That led him to develop a new slogan; soon it was appearing in Marshall Fields adverts on billboards and in local newspapers, as well as on huge banners above the entrances and display windows of the store itself. Hurry up and shop, they subconsciously urged passersby, because there are "Only X Shopping Days Until Christmas".

Under Selfridge's dynamic leadership the Marshall Field retail store went from strength to strength. More innovations were introduced. Goods were taken down from high shelves and displayed at waist height on tables and counters, creating a more friendly and inviting appearance. The spartan ladies' cloakrooms were remodeled, and a store restaurant – the first in Chicago – was opened. Previously, the display windows had been dark at night; now they were kept illuminated so passersby could see what was on display at any time.[x] Those displays were far more appealing, too, with more naturally posed mannequins displaying complimentary items. These were all Selfridge's ideas, the product of an energy that earned him the nickname "Mile-a-minute Harry" among the store's staff. At the same time, he was also pursuing his private life, and his success there was just as great as what he'd achieved at Marshall Field.

CHAPTER 3: MRS. SELFRIDGE

The first member of the Buckingham family to make a mark in the New World was Alvah Buckingham. He was born in March 1791, at Ballston Springs, New York, and few details of his parents are known. It's reasonable to assume from their surname that they or their immediate ancestors were from England. When Alvah was a young boy the family moved to Cooperstown, then in 1799 struck out to the west. By 1802, they were settled in Athens County, in what would later become the township of Carthage. The growing settlement had a school and the Buckinghams could afford to send Alvah and his two older brothers there; education was far from universal at the time. Outside of school they helped on the family farm and hunted in the surrounding woods. From what's known about society at the time we can guess that the oldest brother would have taken over the farm in time, but the other two had different ideas. In 1812 Alvah and his brother Ebenezer moved to Putnam, near Zanesville, and set up a grain shipping business on the banks of the Muskingum River. The Muskingum flows into the Ohio River at Marietta, and the Ohio in turn empties into the Mississippi, so E. Buckingham & Co. could ship the grain they bought to a huge expanse of the expanding nation.

Unfortunately, Ebenezer Buckingham died in 1832. Alvah reorganized the company and changed the name to A. Buckingham & Co, and took on a partner named Solomon Sturges to help him run the business. In 1845 there was another reorganization; the old company was dissolved and a new one, Buckingham & Sturges, formed. They helped build the first grain elevator in Chicago in 1851 and opened branches in New York and Toledo, which were run by Buckingham's oldest sons. One of these, Benjamin Buckingham, later took over the firm's business in Chicago, which by the late 1850s was immense. In addition to their own shipping and storage business, they had a contract with the Illinois Central Railroad to do all their grain warehousing for the next ten years,[xi] and an increasing number of other major contracts throughout the East Coast and Midwest.

Benjamin Buckingham and his brother Philo steadily took on larger roles in running the Chicago operations, and thanks to their considerable wealth, also became notable figures in upper-class Chicago society. Benjamin married another member of that society, Martha Euretta

Potwin, and on July 5, 1960 their first daughter was born. Rosalie Amelia Buckingham was brought up from the start in a way that suited her for life among the industrial aristocracy, but sadly when she was only four years old, her father died suddenly. That was a tragedy, but in financial terms at least the family was secure; Rose, her younger sister Anna and their mother all inherited large sums from Benjamin, more than adequate to let them live in the same grand style as they had enjoyed so far.

The rich at the time were educated at home or in private schools, and a tour of Europe was seen as an essential part of a girl's development. Between 1873 and 1879 Rose, Anna and Martha made several trips to various European countries, where the girls studied languages and music.[xii] She may also have studied business, because a few years later she started investing in high-end Chicago real estate. In 1883, she bought a row of plots along South Harper Avenue in the Hyde Park neighborhood, which would become part of the city in 1889, with the intention of building a row of luxury houses. To help with this she went looking for an architect and found one of Chicago's leading building experts, Solon Spencer Beman. Beman was a controversial figure in the city, having designed a planned workers' community for the Pullman Railroad Company, but his talent was never in doubt. He later went on to create Chicago's famous Grand Central Station. Now Rose asked him to start designing houses on several plots along her property.

While Beman set to work on what would become known as the Rosalie Villas, Rose herself went travelling again. From 1884 to 1888 she and her family spent time in Europe and the Middle East. Their catalogue of destinations was far more extensive than most wealthy Americans visited, and included Britain, Germany, the Scandinavian countries, Russia, Turkey, Egypt and the Holy Land. In the fall of 1888, Rose returned to Chicago and, in addition to re-entering the social scene, brought herself up to date on the progress of her building project. Sometime later that year she met Harry Selfridge at a function and a relationship began to develop.

By now, Rose was 28 years old, and by the standards of the time she'd already left it quite late to find a husband. Most women of her social class were presented as debutantes in their late teens or early twenties, attending a series of organized social events where they would meet "suitable" young men, and the majority of them were married by the time they were 22 or 23 years old. Rose was still single, and there is some evidence she was sensitive about this; when she applied for a new passport in 1888 she gave her year of birth as 1866, subtracting six years from her real age. Her age wasn't a problem for Selfridge, though – at 30 he was past the normal marriage age himself, so he and Rose were a good match.

Selfridge's career was also progressing well. On January 1, 1890 Marshall Field made him a junior partner in the firm, hugely increasing both his income and his status. He was no longer a mere employee, but part-owner of a major business.

Harry Selfridge and Rose Buckingham married in Chicago's Central Church on November 11, 1890. They didn't find a home of their own immediately; instead they moved in with Rose's sister, Anna Buckingham Chandler and her husband. Lois Selfridge also moved in; she would live with the couple all through their married life, an arrangement that was quite common across all social classes at the time if one spouse's mother was widowed. In this case, both their fathers were dead, and Martha Buckingham was already living there. The newlyweds didn't plan to stay there in the long term, however; they soon began looking for a home of their own.

By this time, Rose's property in Hyde Park was fully developed, with a number of other prominent architects including Beman having designed houses there. The area had become a planned development in a beautifully landscaped setting, with over 40 villas and cottages. Building a home there was an option, but they decided against it. Meanwhile, they set about increasing the size of their family. Sadly, their first son, Chandler, died shortly after he was born in 1891, but four more children followed over the next ten years. Rosalie Jr. was born in 1893, Violette in 1897, Gordon Jr. in 1900 and Beatrice in 1901.[xiii]

The Selfridges now had a secure place in Chicago society, but they weren't confining themselves to the city. Shortly after they married they began looking for a country home as well. They settled on Lake Geneva in Walworth County, Wisconsin; with easy access from Chicago by train this small town had become a popular vacation resort for the city's wealthier inhabitants, many of whom had built homes there, and the couple had been spending their summers there since their marriage. In fact their first son, Chandler, was buried in the resort's churchyard. It was a place they both loved.

At that time most of the lake frontage hadn't yet been bought up, and Harry managed to buy a plot. It was a vacant plot of course, but he already knew what he wanted to put on it. Chicago's biggest event of 1893 was the World's Fair held in the city, which had attracted more than 27 million visitors. It featured nearly 200 buildings built by representatives from 46 countries, many of them built to show off traditional architectural styles, and a huge range of other attractions. The first Ferris wheel was built there, part of a carnival area centered on the Midway Plaisance park – that's why the sideshow area of a carnival is now called the midway in the USA. The first commercial movie theater was part of the fair, as was the first moving walkway. What had caught the eye of the Selfridges, however, was one of the national pavilions. It had been built by the island nation of Ceylon, now Sri Lanka, in a traditional style. Along with most of the other buildings, it was scheduled for demolition when the fair ended but instead Harry bought it, had it dismantled, then shipped it to Lake Geneva and had it rebuilt on his plot. It quickly became known as Ceylon Court.[xiv]

As much as the Selfridges liked their lakeside home, it was only a short-term solution. Like most of the other temporary buildings it was built from a compound called "staff," a mix of cement, plaster and jute fibers that formed a sort of early drywall, and it wouldn't survive many seasons in the Midwestern climate. If they wanted to have a permanent home by the lake – and they did – they would need to build a more durable one.

There was another vacant plot right next to Ceylon Court, a large one with 300 feet of shore. Harry managed to buy that one too, and on it he had a house built. It was a remarkable structure, both in design and appearance. From the outside it was a large English-style mock Tudor mansion, with the ground floor built from local stone and the upper floors in timber and white plaster. Underneath the traditional appearance, however, was a steel structural frame; it was probably the first example of fireproof construction used in a private home.[xv] As a tribute to his wife, roses were used throughout the property as a decorative theme; even the iron fence posts that surrounded it each had a rose cast into the metal. It was a beautiful and luxurious house and both of the Selfridges loved it. As a name, they gave it a composite of their own names: Harrose Hall.

Harrose Hall was completed in 1899 and instantly became a favorite of the whole family. For decades afterwards, the couple and their children would return to the house every chance they had, even if it meant travelling an extra thousand miles just to spend a day there. Until it was finally demolished in 1975, it remained one of the most spectacular and comfortable houses in Lake Geneva.

The same year Harrose Hall was completed, the Selfridges finally found themselves a home of their own in Chicago. It was an imposing Victorian villa at 117 Lake Shore Drive (now 1430 North Lake Shore Drive) that had been built in 1890 for an elderly widow. She had died in 1898 and the house subsequently came on the market. The Selfridges managed to buy it for $100,000. At the time the average cost of a family home in the USA was less than $5,000.

By the turn of the century, Selfridge was finally running out of things to do at Marshall Field. He was a very wealthy man by this time and had huge prestige among Chicago's businessmen for the improvements he'd introduced to the retail store, improvements that were rapidly being adopted across the nation as competitors scrambled to keep up with this new way of doing things. For the moment Marshall Field was leading the industry. Now, Harry started to wonder how well he could do if he could start with a clean slate, instead of having to work within the framework of a long-established company. In 1903, he decided to find out.

In early 1904, Selfridge sold his interest in Marshall Field & Co. and used the money as startup capital for his own department store. He bought another Chicago firm, Schlesinger & Mayer, which already had a large store, and set about reshaping it in his own image. The store was closed down, completely overhauled then reopened as H.G. Selfridge & Co. The store was a success, but for some reason not a satisfying one. Only two months after opening it Selfridge sold up – at a handsome profit – to Carson Pirie Scott & Co. Still aged only 48, he retired and set out to find ways to keep himself amused. He and his family spent much of their time at Harrose Hall. Harry bought a steam yacht to sail on the lake, although he quickly grew bored with it – probably because the lake was less than eight miles long and barely a mile wide. He played golf. And, sometimes together with Rose and the children, he traveled.

CHAPTER 4: LONDON

London in the 21st century is one of the world's largest, wealthiest cities. Only two US cities – New York and Los Angeles – have a larger population in their metro areas, and LA only beats it out by a few hundred thousand. More than fifteen million people live in London's sprawl. The city itself dwarfs Los Angeles and comes within 100,000 of NYC's 8.4 million people. London is also the world's second financial center after New York, and handles a more diverse range of trades. It's the most significant capital city in Europe and a major center for education. London is an important place.

And that's now. In the first decade of the 20th century it was, quite simply, a city with no equal. The British Empire was at the absolute height of its size, wealth and power. The Royal Navy dominated every one of the world's oceans, protecting a vast trade network that brought in Canadian gold, South African diamonds, Indian hardwood and Chinese silk, along with raw materials and manufactured goods from a quarter of the world's land surface. Much of that trade and the wealth it created flowed into London. The city was already immense, bigger than any other in the world; over 6.5 million people lived there, almost twice as many as in New York.[xvi] Dozens of nations followed British law and had the British monarch as head of state; dozens more were ruled directly from the Colonial Office on Whitehall, the broad street that houses the main departments of the British government. There were more local-currency millionaires in London than in the entire USA – and £1 million was worth nearly $5 million. Moscow, Istanbul and Madrid still ruled their decaying empires, Paris was the global center of fashion, Berlin's militarism was starting to tilt the European balance of power and the big US cities were fast-growing centers of business and manufacturing, but London was the world's leading city. Rose Selfridge had been there on her earlier European trips, but her husband hadn't and now he had the time and money to make up for that. In 1906 he sailed to England for a vacation and his first destination was the capital. Unsurprisingly, when he got there Harry went shopping.

London's been a good city to go shopping in for quite awhile. In fact, nobody knows exactly how long it's been one for but it's probably something over 2,000 years. The remains of Roman shops have been found[xvii] and while their stock is long gone – either cleared out by departing owners or looted by invaders – we know that the Roman Empire had a lively retail sector. Compared to most people 2,000 years ago, even a working class Roman home contained a huge range of belongings and unlike their contemporaries most Romans didn't make many of their own possessions. Instead they bought the output of slave-powered factories that shipped their goods all over the empire; any Roman town had a range of shops selling good produced hundreds, even thousands of miles away. The retail sector declined after the fall of Rome. The Saxons, who began conquering Britain in the 5th century, were stolid farmers who lived in small communities and avoided the crumbling Roman city, and the Norsemen who followed them a few centuries later didn't really seem to understand the concept of buying things – they tended to just pillage them.

By the Middle Ages, the city's retail trade was expanding again. Daily or weekly markets were held in most public squares and the streets were lined with specialty shops selling clothing, jewelry, furnishings, weapons and much more. Shops were scattered, though; there was no concept of a shopping district, and most were run out the ground floor of the owner's house. In 1565, Sir Thomas Gresham decided to change all that.

Sir Thomas was the son of Sir Richard Gresham, a prominent merchant and former Lord Mayor of London who also served as a financial adviser to King Henry VIII. As a boy, Thomas became a merchant's apprentice for eight years, working for his uncle, and then studied at the University of Cambridge. At age 24, he moved to Antwerp, working as a merchant in the family business and also acting as the king's agent. He survived three changes of monarch and became an adviser to Queen Elizabeth I, carrying out both financial and political missions for her. Then, in 1565, he proposed building a new center of commerce for London, modeled on the great exchange in Antwerp. His vision was for a place that dealt with all levels of commerce, where merchants could make deals in comfortable, professional surroundings, and crowds of shoppers would be attracted by an array of small retailers. The Royal Exchange was completed in 1571 and Queen Elizabeth opened it in person; it contained bars and coffee shops, perfumers, clothes shops and sellers of high-quality accessories. The best way to describe it is a 16th century shopping mall.

The Royal Exchange burned down – along with most of London – between September 2 and September 5, 1666. An accident in a bakery, combined with a long hot summer that had turned the city's mostly wooden buildings to tinder sparked the Great Fire, devastating almost all of the old walled city and many outlying residential areas. It's estimated that over 80 per cent of London's homes were burned out. London had been destroyed before, however, and always rises from the ruins. Within weeks, thousands of laborers and architects were hard at work building a new city, one with safer, more durable stone houses and wider streets to replace the warren of narrow lanes that had existed before. One of them, laid out along the route of an old Roman military road, soon came to be called Oxford Street.

A huge new wave of building and modernization began in the 19th century and accelerated under the young, energetic new Queen, Victoria. Streets were redeveloped with imposing multi-story stone buildings, many of which still stand. Some of them were retail premises, including department stores. The way they were distributed was strange, though. Oxford Street quickly became one of London's premier shopping locations, with a dazzling array of high class shops including the royal jeweler, Garrards. There was one omission though. London's biggest stores were scattered elsewhere: Harrods and Harvey Nichols in Knightsbridge, Fortnum & Mason in Piccadilly and Liberty on Regent Street. When Harry and Rose wandered along Oxford Street in early 1906, looking into the shop window displays as they went, they didn't see a department store. Given his experience in that area, Harry found it a conspicuous omission. Almost immediately he started wondering if he could do something about that.

Department stores are a British invention. As the Industrial Revolution gathered speed in the late 18th century, it caused huge changes in British society, starting a massive flow of people from the countryside into the growing towns. At the same time, it sparked the beginnings of a consumer society. Factory and mill workers weren't wealthy, but they still had a lot more disposable income than they'd had as farm laborers. They began to acquire more belongings and a range of shops and street markets sprang up to meet the demand. These markets were often loud, rowdy places though, and weren't attractive to the relatively new but fast-growing middle class. This group, who had even more money to spend, were looking for stores that could supply the high-quality products they were looking for in a more comfortable atmosphere. Merchants soon started looking for ways to provide this and quite soon they hit on the solution.

Harding, Howell & Co. opened on London's exclusive Pall Mall in 1796. It was laid out on one large single floor, unlike a modern department store, but its retail space was divided into four sections by partitions of glass and wood panels. One of these dealt in ladies' clothing, another in gloves and hats, while a third sold elegant clocks and home accessories. Immediately inside the entrance were furs and fashionable fans; this was an interesting placement of luxury goods, probably designed to attract as wide a range of shoppers as possible by offering a range of desirable items at a selection of prices. Whether someone entered Harding, Howell & Co. to look at an inexpensive fan or a mink coat, once they were through the door they would find plenty more to interest them. It's a principle that department stores still use today.

Harding, Howell & Co. quickly became a success and other retailers copied and expanded the concept. Kendals in Manchester had started in 1796 as a drapery business but soon expanded into multiple floors, each selling different kinds of goods, and by 1836 had taken over a second building across the street; the two were connected by a shop-lined arcade under the street. Harrods, a Knightsbridge grocery, also expanded and by the end of the 19th century the current, enormous building was under construction. Arthur Lasenby Liberty opened his eponymous store on Regent Street in 1875, in a distinctive mock-Tudor building it still occupies, pitched at the upper levels of society; its departments, split into a huge number of small display rooms, sold only the most prestigious brands. By the time the Selfridges visited London, the city had several of Europe's leading department stores; it just didn't have one on its main shopping street.

Of course Selfridge did find London's department stores, but he remained unimpressed. Perhaps because they included some of the oldest examples in the world they seemed old-fashioned compared to what Marshall Field had become. The staff showed many of the old attitudes he'd worked so hard to overcome in Chicago and while the stock was usually extremely high quality it wasn't presented anywhere near as well as it could have been. Clearly in London, shopping was still something you did when you needed something; at Marshall Field and the American stores that were following its example, it had become an enjoyable experience in its own right.

Selfridge had retired two years earlier, having made enough money to easily last a lifetime, but already he was bored. Before too long, he started contemplating the challenge of opening a new store. He knew he could do that – he'd done it with Harry G. Selfridge & Co. – but this would be a bigger task. Instead of buying an existing building and going into business for himself in a town that already knew his reputation, he would be attempting to start from scratch and revolutionize shopping in a city with its own traditions, its own established brands and its own very different way of doing things. There was a lot that could go wrong. That probably just made the challenge even more tempting.

One of the problems with London's existing department stores was their old-fashioned way of doing things. That could be dealt with using the methods he'd introduced in Chicago. The other problem was location. He believed the best place for a new store would be on Oxford Street, which attracted more shoppers than anywhere else. The older stores were scattered through the city center. That didn't matter much to someone who wanted to buy a suit from Harrods or curtain fabric from Liberty, because those people knew what they were looking for and made a trip specifically to get it. Selfridge believed that way of doing things missed a lot of potential customers, though. If a store could attract passersby with its window displays and tempt a decent percentage of them to come inside, it could generate a lot of impulse sales. For that to work it had to be in a busy location, and Oxford Street was ideal for that.

Today, the east end of Oxford Street, where it meets Tottenham Court Road, is a disappointingly generic urban area. At street level it's an identikit parade of budget cell phone dealers, ethnic fast food joints and retail chains – everything from Jessops Photography to health food brand Holland & Barrett. Keep your eyes down and it could be any street in any British town. Look up, though, and the architecture gives you a clue as to what it once was. The handsome three and four-floor buildings, built in classic Victorian style from pale stone and red brick, have weathered well. The occasional post-War intrusion replaces bomb damage – Oxford Street was bombed by the Nazis in 1940, and again by the IRA in 1973 – but mostly, once you get above the ground floor, it's a very elegant Victorian street. In most of the buildings only the ground floor is used for business; the upper levels are residential apartments. In 1906, this was very much the fashionable end of Oxford Street, and property there was very much in demand. The cost of buying and clearing a plot big enough to hold a department store was out of the question, even for Selfridge.

Instead, he started looking around the west end of the street. This area was much less fashionable for shops, which was a disadvantage, but it had its own attractions. In the west Oxford Street ends at Marble Arch, one of London's traditional landmarks. The arch itself stands at one corner of Hyde Park, which attracts many visitors, and in addition to being the end of Oxford Street it's also the end of one of London's many millionaires' rows, Park Lane. Overall, there was enough going on along the western end to guarantee a good supply of passersby. Of course, Selfridge's vision was of a store that would be a popular attraction all on its own, and with the right amenities he thought it could pull in a good share of the crowds around Marble Arch.

After returning home, Selfridge sat down to do some serious planning. It didn't take him long to decide that the idea was practical. He could afford to build and launch a store near Marble Arch, and keep it going until it began to make a profit. Retirement was over. Returning to London, he began looking for a suitable location. It didn't take him long to find one. He managed to buy a full block on the north side of Oxford Street, running from Orchard Street to Duke Street - a plot 180 yards long and 150 yards deep. Photos from the time show a row of mismatched four-story buildings in a variety of styles, with shops at street level and a mixture of office space and apartments above. There was no way the existing buildings could be converted into a department store, but that wasn't part of the plan anyway. Selfridge had rejuvenated one store and founded another, but both times he'd done so in an existing building. This time he had the chance to start with a blank slate and he intended to make the most of it. Within months of

Selfridge buying it the entire block had been razed to the ground and a huge excavation was underway to make space for the foundations and basement levels of the new store.

In addition to its size the site of the new store had another major advantage. It was directly opposite one of the entrances to Bond Street Station, part of the London Underground network. Today two lines run through Bond Street Station, since the first section of the Jubilee Line was built in 1971. In 1906, there was only one line there but it was the Central Line, the busiest route on the whole network. That suited Selfridge's plans perfectly – every day thousands of people would pour out of that station entrance onto Oxford Street, and the first thing they saw would be his spectacular new store.

And it was certainly going to be spectacular. In total Selfridge was investing £400,000 in the new store. In 1906, one Pound Sterling was worth about $4.85, so the total sum was close to two million dollars. Adjusted into 2014 dollars, that's a billion dollar project, and the investment paid off. Selfridge would have liked to build the biggest department store in the country but that wasn't feasible; Harrods had opened their new building in 1905 and it was enormous; its sales floors had a total area of more than a million square feet. More than a century later it's still Europe's largest department store by a long way; the runner-up, Berlin's KaDeWe, comes in at a mere 650,000 square feet. Harrods could build such a huge structure because of their location but Selfridge was constrained by the street grid in central London. The largest he could manage was 540,000 square feet of retail space, still enough to be (both then and now) the second largest department store in the UK. That was an impressive achievement on its own, but to make it an even more attractive place to visit he carefully applied every one of the lessons he'd learned in Chicago.

For the actual design of the building Selfridge brought in an American architect, Daniel Burnham. It was an obvious choice; in addition to New York's famous Flatiron Building Burnham had designed the Marshall Field store, so he and Selfridge were already acquainted. Burnham had a solid understanding of how a department store should be built and that, combined with Selfridge's genius for retail, gave the pair all the skills they needed to come up with something special. What they had in mind was a building like nothing London had ever seen before.

The two building materials most associated with London are Portland stone, a high quality pale gray limestone, and the ubiquitous red brick. Between them these materials give the city center much of its character; most prominent pre-20th century buildings are constructed from one or both of them. To fit in with the surroundings, Burnham and Selfridge decided to stay with them, but they were looking for a radically different style. Because London doesn't face any earthquake hazard, large buildings of brick (with or without stone facing) or of stone blocks are very durable, but the characteristics of the materials put a limit on the way they can be designed; to give enough structural rigidity, the size of windows and other openings has to be kept relatively small. That can be seen from looking at Harrods. Although the massive building has hundreds of windows they're not very large, and most of the façade is stone.

London's famously damp weather means that in pre-central heating days the natives didn't see this as a problem; thick stone or brick walls are a much better insulator than a pane of window glass. However, Selfridge wanted the store to be as bright and airy as he could manage and there was a way to do that. Again Burnham turned out to be the idea choice. He'd been able to build the Flatiron because New York had changed its building codes in 1892. Before then the law required that buildings had to use solid masonry for its fireproof properties. With the change he could now use steel frame construction, making the 22-story Flatiron possible. Selfridge also knew the benefits of steel framed buildings after his experiment at Harrose Hall, and was keen to use the same technology for the new store. That would allow much larger windows, because they were no longer limited by the width of a stone lintel. There was only one problem: London's building codes hadn't been updated.

Building regulations in the capital were set by London City Council, and the last major update had been in 1844. Earthquakes might not have been a problem in London but fire was, and after the city's incineration in 1666, planners were always conscious of the danger. Wooden buildings had almost vanished from the city after the Great Fire, and masonry – and, later, brick – were prized for their unwillingness to burn. Even if a brick building did burn out, the walls would help to contain the fire and prevent it spreading. Steel frame construction was new, and before the City Council would let Selfridge and Burnham build their store they would have to show that, in the event of a fire, it wouldn't collapse and spill burning debris into the surrounding blocks. Selfridge and

Burnham started looking for a precedent, and they also found an engineer who could design the building's frame. Sven Bylander was a Swedish structural specialist who'd learned about steel as a draftsman in a shipyard then applied his knowledge to buildings in Germany and the USA.[xviii] Now he searched London for any sign of steel buildings – and he got lucky. At the time, the city was a major commercial port and the Docklands district, now a middle to high income residential area, was a maze of docks and warehouses. Many of the warehouses were brick, but some of the more recent ones were steel-framed. The owners had managed to persuade the City Council that this method had a lot of advantages – greater interior space being a major one – and was safe enough. If it could be used for something as notoriously flammable as a warehouse there was no reason to rule it out for a department store, so Bylander prepared some initial plans and made contact with the Metropolitan Buildings Office.

British Buildings Offices are famous for their slow-moving conservative approach to new innovations, but Bylander seems to have been luckier than most applicants. Perhaps the planners were eager to catch up with New York; in any case they were willing to consider the plans and soon Bylander was working with them to solve their remaining worries. They agreed on a deep foundation of brick piers, supporting a total of eight floors – three basement levels and five above ground. The structure would be built around a steel frame with the piers extending up around its perimeter; the steel would support the concrete floor slabs at each level. Externally the piers were to be clad in Portland stone; the spaces between them would hold cast iron window frames, allowing for a huge area of glazing. Decorative columns from the second to fourth floors were added to give the building a suitably dramatic appearance. The Buildings Office still had some worries about fire, so they ruled that no single space inside the building could be larger than 450,000 cubic feet.[xix] Bylander agreed, but he hoped this rule would be relaxed in the future (it was) so he made sure the necessary partitions would be easily removable. Again, the steel frame helped; the partitions met the required fire resistance standard but were kept as light as possible and were supported by the framework. They had no structural role in the building and could be removed without damaging its strength. The maximum size of internal doorway was also doubled, to allow 12 by 12-foot openings; this allowed daylight to penetrate into the center of each floor even with the partitions in place. In 1907, the Buildings Office approved the new design and construction began.

Yet again, the chosen construction method paid off. Selfridge wanted to get the store open as soon as possible, but putting up such a large building would take time. Harrods, built using more traditional methods, had taken eleven years to complete. Because the steel framework was built in prefabricated sections that were assembled on site, however, it was possible to build it in sections. The frontage of the store was split into "bays", each separated by a brick pier; the plan was for 20 bays in total, ten each side of the main entrance. To meet Selfridge's initial time scale, the first phase consisted of building nine bays at the Duke Street end of the store, complete with a temporary entrance. The resulting store was only a quarter the size of Harrods, but Burnham and Bylander managed to build it in a year and a half.

With the truncated building complete, it was time for Selfridge to take over. This was his chance to put all his ideas into effect with no constraints imposed by the location. One of those ideas was about space. Previous department stores had been divided into a series of distinct rooms, with Liberty being an extreme example. The new one turned that on its head. Each floor was still split up into departments but, except where the fire partitions made it necessary, that wouldn't be done by walls. Instead elaborate displays would mark the borders between one department and the next, with leaving sightlines as open as possible. Thanks to the big, permanently open doors in the partitions – Bylander pioneered the use of concertina shutters to close them when necessary – it was often possible to look from one end of a floor to another. This gave the store an open feeling, and left the prominent displays visible to tempt people into other departments. To aid this effect Selfridge even redesigned the internal furniture. Most store counters at the time were designed to be at mid-chest height; instead these, and as many other items as possible, would be kept to waist level.[xx] Again, this added to the feeling of spaciousness.

Selfridge's efforts didn't end at making the sales floors look good. There were nine elevators throughout the building to speed customers between floors, as well as eight staircases for the more nervous. Escalators were already in existence but weren't very popular; unlike the familiar modern design with its smoothly sliding metal steps, the early models were simply leather belts with wooden cleats to stop the passengers' feet from slipping. When Harrods installed one in 1898, they famously offered free smelling salts and cognac at the top to revive nervous riders.[xxi] That was a gimmick to make the store look daring and cutting-edge, but many people really did feel uncomfortable about using them so Selfridge stuck with the more acceptable elevators.

The in-store restaurants were also part of Selfridge's plan. Eating out in central London can get expensive quickly, and the middle-class shoppers Selfridge wanted to attract would be reluctant to visit the fast food shops of the time – jellied eel stands or pie shops, which were often filled with terrifyingly drunk laborers. An elegant but inexpensive restaurant in a central location had the potential to bring in a lot of diners, and if it brought them into the store so much the better. Several restaurants were located throughout the store, each catering to a different type of customer. A conservatory on the roof terrace housed an upscale formal restaurant, while others catered to families, fashionable young people or shoppers with limited time on their hands. A tearoom offered quality cakes, and small stands in the food hall gave shoppers a sample of the many delicacies on offer there.

Selfridge's grand concept even took account of London's place as the center of a huge empire and its importance for international trade. Although he expected most of his customers to be Londoners or visitors from elsewhere in Britain, he went out of his way to make overseas visitors feel welcome. There were special rooms for American, French, German and "Colonial" guests, with décor and music chosen to make them feel at home. A library gave the studious a place to relax. For everyone else there was a "silence room" which offered comfortable chairs, double glazing and soft ambient lights.[xxii] Every feature was carefully devised to bring people into the store and persuade them to stay as long as possible.

By early 1909, the store was finished and ready for the public. Staff was recruited – a total of 1,400 employees were taken on.[xxiii] All of them had to be trained in Harry's new way of doing things. Those who would be working on the sales floors were taught the correct way to interact with customers – helpful, but not pushy. If a customer looked around for assistance there should be someone close by, but nobody would be badgered by hard-selling staff. Selfridge had his own reasons for disliking this approach. Not long after he'd first come to London he'd been browsing in a store when a floorwalker approached him. "Is Sir intending to buy something?" the man asked in an impeccable British accent. Selfridge replied, "No, I'm just looking." Instantly the good manners vanished – "Then 'op it, mate."[xxiv] That wasn't how he wanted his own customers to be treated, so floorwalkers weren't part of his staff requirements.

Employees were also taught how to demonstrate products to customers. Electrical appliances were starting to become more common at the time and the store would carry a wide range of them, and Selfridge believed that showing them in action was a good way to encourage sales.

In the early weeks of 1909, the London newspapers were flooded with adverts for the new store. For the time the publicity campaign was huge and elaborate, offering tantalizing hints about the store's luxury and the range of goods available inside. By early March, London was buzzing with excitement. When Selfridge's opened on

March 15, 1909, it was an elaborately choreographed spectacle. As the minutes ticked away toward the announced opening time crowds formed in the street outside. The doors were closed; silk curtains covered every one of the big plate glass windows. Then, at precisely 9:00am, a bugler stepped out onto the balcony above the entrance and blew a fanfare. Simultaneously, the doors swung open and every one of the curtains rose together, uncovering displays of fashionable clothing modeled by mannequins in lifelike poses. By the end of the day 90,000 people had been counted entering the store.[xxv] Selfridge's had been an instant success.[xxvi]

CHAPTER 5: THE GOLDEN YEARS

The five years after the new store opened were probably the high point of Harry Selfridge's life. He had achieved yet another massive business success, creating a revolutionary new retail outlet in the world's most important city. He had his wife and four children. The public admired him and his fellow businessmen held him in immense respect. The plans were ready for the expansion of the store to its full planned size and the money he would need to carry out the work was accumulating rapidly. He managed to persuade the General Post Office, who ran Britain's telephone network at the time, to give the store the telephone number 1. Anyone who wanted to be put through to Selfridge's simply had to call the operator and ask for Garrard, which in the days before direct dial made it much easier to get through. Flushed with success, Harry even went as far as to suggest cutting a tunnel from the store's basement level to Bond Street Station, which he proposed should be renamed Selfridge's Station. That was a step too far even for him – the idea was shot down by combined public and official opposition. The attempt didn't dent the store's popularity, though.

With the store open, Harry had been joined in England by Rose and their children. As a family residence, he bought Lansdowne House, a large mansion on Berkeley Square. It was a spectacular house, designed by the famous architect Robert Adam, and had belonged to three former British prime ministers. Rose loved the house and enthusiastically joined in with London society, giving harp performances – she was an excellent harpist – and hosting parties that became hugely popular.

What was less popular, certainly with Rose, was Harry's womanizing. His sudden prominence in London society, and his huge wealth, attracted a stream of curious women and he found it very hard to resist them. He had a less than discreet affair with Syrie Wellcome, the estranged wife of an American pharmaceuticals millionaire. His name was linked with Russian ballerina Anna Pavlova and a string of other prominent society women. Rose never said a word, probably in the interests of domestic harmony, but often Selfridge's latest real or assumed conquest was the talk of the town.

There were other low points as well. In 1911, the family was on holiday in the Lake District, in the north of England. It's one of the most beautiful parts of the country but the roads are often steep and winding, weaving a dangerous path through the valleys carved out by the last Ice Age. Descending one hill toward the resort town of Ambleside on Lake Windermere, their car's brakes failed and the car raced downhill out of control. Finally it came off the road and slammed into the side of a house, throwing its occupants onto the ground. Harry suffered serious cuts and a concussion that left him unconscious for almost a day. Rose suffered two broken bones in one arm, and Harry's mother Lois and daughter Rosalie Junior were both badly bruised. The accident dampened Rose's enthusiasm for life in England, and she began to make more frequent trips back to Chicago to visit her family. Soon, a bigger tragedy would make even that dangerous.

The First World War broke out on July 28, 1914, after a period of tension between the great European powers. Within a year it would expand out of control to become the largest conflict the world had yet seen, but at first, its impact on London was limited. Between Britain's huge Royal Navy and the powerful armies of France and Russia it was expected that Germany and her allies would be defeated within months, and the country was swept by a wave of patriotic fervor. In most respects, life went on as normal, though. The British Army was an all-volunteer force and relatively small, so it didn't disrupt society when a large part of it was sent to France. Most people in London went right on with their lives and business at Selfridge's continued to boom. When the Army began recruiting on a large scale later that year it was another boost for many retailers. While soldiers were issued everything they would need, officers were expected to buy several items themselves, such as a handgun and binoculars, and there were many other optional pieces of equipment they could purchase. For example, the Burberry trench coat was a popular, and authorized, replacement for the heavy woolen greatcoat the Army provided. Selfridge's was the ideal place to stock up on high quality items before boarding a train to the Channel ports. By late 1915 thousands of men were dying every day in the trenches of the Western Front, but Selfridge's continued to prosper.

In 1916 the war started to extend its tentacles further afield. Germany had built a fleet of Zeppelin airships and they could carry bombs. Their payload was neither very large nor very accurate, and in fact in the early years of the war the Kaiser had forbidden any raids on London, but by the end of 1914, the enormous craft were roaming over the cities of Poland, Greece and Belgium at night dropping bombs. Nobody could say how long London's apparent immunity would last, and Harry decided to look for a place away from the huge target of the city.[xxvii] He found Highcliffe Castle, a Dorset mansion about 80 miles southwest of London. Despite its medieval name and appearance, Highcliffe was actually a Georgian villa, built between 1831 and 1835, but large amounts of salvaged medieval stonework from two old Norman churches had been used in its construction. It was a huge home with extensive grounds including elaborate formal gardens, and had earned some publicity in 1907 when Kaiser Wilhelm II – now the figurehead of Britain's enemies, but formerly a friendly foreign relative of Queen Victoria – had spent three weeks there recovering from an illness. Two stained glass windows presented by the German leader had been installed in the house to mark the event. The recipient of these gifts, Edward Montagu-Stuart-Wortley, was an officer in the British Army and was now a Major General serving in France. He didn't particularly need Highcliffe at the time, and owned other homes in any case, so when Selfridge offered to lease it from him he was happy to accept. In fact, Selfridge treated the house as if he'd bought it, having substantial improvements carried out. A new kitchen, modern bathrooms and a central heating system were some of the more notable changes he made.[xxviii]

Meanwhile, Rose was getting involved in the war effort. As an American citizen neither Britain nor her own government would let her get directly involved in war work, but the Red Cross had no such scruples and were busily recruiting volunteers. The couple's two older daughters, Rosalie and Violette, joined the Red Cross and worked at Christchurch Hospital. Rose also signed up but her skills took her in a different direction. Unlike today, most people in 1916 couldn't drive, and there was a desperate shortage of ambulance drivers. Many American men signed up to help transport the wounded from the front line back to field hospitals in France; to free up more men for this vital role women who could drive were recruited to work in England. Rose could drive, so she found herself in a Red Cross uniform carrying wounded men from the Channel ports to hospitals around southern England.

Meanwhile Harry, still busy running the store, had even grander plans for the family. Highcliffe was only a lease, but he had decided to acquire a permanent home on the picturesque Dorset coast and he started making enquiries about buying Hengistbury Head, a mile-long promontory two miles west of Highcliffe. The Head and the sandbar that ran from its end enclosed a natural harbor, and Selfridge planned to build himself a grand castle-style home there. However, these plans were interrupted in 1917 by a new development in the war.

Since fighting broke out in 1914, US President Woodrow Wilson had been sticking to a policy of non-interference in European affairs. Public opinion was split at first, with one segment of the population supporting Britain while Americans of German, Swedish and Irish descent, along with a majority of women and religious leaders, favoring neutrality or even an alliance with Germany. As the war went on and reports of German atrocities against Belgian civilians (most of which later proved to be false) started to filter through opinion began to swing more solidly toward the British side, especially after the famous transatlantic liner RMS *Lusitania* was sunk by a German U-Boat in 1915. Wilson officially maintained neutrality but began making large loans available to Britain and France to help them finance their war efforts. Finally, in early 1917, two events came together in a perfect storm of diplomatic outrage. First, Germany announced that unrestricted submarine warfare against ships sailing to Britain – which had been suspended after the *Lusitania* sinking – would be resumed. As American ships were still trading freely with the British, that made it almost inevitable that some would be sunk. Secondly, British Naval Intelligence intercepted and decoded a telegram from Germany to their embassy in Mexico City. This ultra-secret message told the ambassador to offer the Mexicans an alliance if the USA entered the war on the British side; the effect would have been to expand the war to North America and open a new front along the US-Mexican border. That would have been the end of the matter, if it wasn't for the British. Realizing the potential of their intercept they immediately handed it to the US embassy in London. At first the ambassador rejected it as a provocation but the British were ready for that, and the Germans had been too clever for their own good. They had actually used US diplomatic channels to send the telegram, persuading the Berlin embassy to accept a coded signal, so the USA had the encrypted text. Now the British simply handed over the cipher key and invited the Americans to read it for themselves. Just to be on the safe side they publicly announced the discovery, although to conceal their codebreaking success they claimed to have broken an older, easier code used by the Mexican telegraph office.

The American public was understandably outraged at the "Zimmermann Telegram" and its revelations of hostile plotting. Pro-German agitators in the USA tried to dismiss it as a British plot, but then the Germans shot themselves spectacularly in the foot. Foreign secretary Arthur Zimmermann, the author of the telegram, held a press conference in Berlin on March 3 at which he admitted it was authentic, but justified himself by saying the alliance would only have gone into effect if the USA joined the war. The timing, from his point of view, was not good. The U-Boats had resumed unrestricted attacks on February 1 and two American ships had already gone to the bottom of the Atlantic. President Wilson proposed using US Navy seamen and guns to defend merchant shipping, a move that was opposed by pacifists in the Senate. That refusal just inflamed public opinion even more and on April 6 a joint session of Congress voted to declare war on Germany. The first units of the US Navy and US Marines were on their way to Europe within weeks.

With their nation now fighting on the Allied side, the Selfridges were more connected to the war than they had been before. Its epic tragedy was soon brought home to them in a dramatic way, though. The British and French (and their German opponents) had been fighting a brutal war in the trenches for three years. They'd learned how the power of machine guns and modern artillery paralyzed movement, and that frontal attacks were simply suicidal. The newly arriving Americans hadn't learned these lessons and thought their new allies were simply timid. Fearing disaster, the British and French commanders recommended that US battalions be distributed among existing Allied divisions as reinforcements, but General John J. Pershing was adamant: his men would fight as US divisions and they would follow US doctrine. That called for frontal assaults, and the result was appalling. The Germans were awed by the bravery of the fresh US troops, but that didn't stop them from mowing them down by the thousand as they charged straight at dug-in German machine guns. It didn't take long before Pershing, who was a talented and flexible officer, realized that the British and French had been right; US doctrine was quickly changed to mirror that of the British. By that time, thousands of American soldiers were dead, however, and many more had been seriously wounded and evacuated to England.

By this time the Selfridges had been in England for eleven years and were well settled there, but they still thought of themselves as Americans. Now hospitals across the country were filled with young men from their homeland. Some were out of the war and would be returning to the USA; others, less seriously wounded, would be rejoining their units. All of them needed someplace they could rest and recover from their injuries, and the military hospitals that were springing up were stretched to the limit. Rose, who'd always been an energetic woman with a great deal of personal initiative, wanted to help them if she could. Of course, she could always continue her ambulance work, but she felt there was more that could be done. Finally, she hit on the idea of creating a rest camp where wounded men could convalesce. The advantage of living in a huge country house was that there was plenty of space for a project like that, and of course they had the money to arrange it. Highcliffe's cricket pavilion was converted into an administration office for the camp, quarters were built for a US Army NCO who would be in charge of discipline and a dozen huts were built to house wounded soldiers. A recreation room offered a range of ways to pass the time: books and games, writing materials for letters home, maps for those who wanted to track the progress of the war and a gramophone with a small library of vinyl disks.[xxix] The facility was grandly named "The Mrs. Gordon Selfridge Convalescent Camp For American Soldiers", and the first wounded men arrived in late 1917. By the end of the war, hundreds of soldiers had passed through it, either to gain the strength needed for the long voyage home through U-Boat infested waters, or as a blessed pause before being thrown back into the carnage of the Western Front. The whole project was organized with Rose's characteristic energy and enthusiasm.

Sadly, though, the convalescent camp was to be Rose's last project. By early 1918 the long stalemate in France was slowly beginning to break down and an Allied victory was at last in sight. On the horizon, however, was an even greater outbreak of death and suffering that over the next two years would come to overshadow the war itself.

CHAPTER 6: TRAGEDY

Influenza, more commonly known by the deceptively harmless name "the flu," has been with us for a very long time. The first person to describe its symptoms was the Greek father of medicine, Hippocrates, writing about 2,400 years ago. It seems to have originated in Europe and sailors carried it with them throughout the great age of exploration. In 1493, shortly after Christopher Columbus arrived in the New World, most of the population of the Antilles was killed by a disease that sounds suspiciously like flu. Major outbreaks continued for centuries, sometimes killing thousands of people. It was an age of plagues, though, and when cholera or typhus could decimate a city's population in a matter of weeks – and where fond memories of the Black Death lingered – flu didn't seem too bad. People had a healthy respect for it, but they thought they knew what the disease was capable of. They were horribly mistaken.

Influenza is normally an unpleasant disease that can put an adult in bed for a week of absolute misery and might kill small children, the elderly or those with respiratory problems. In January 1918, a different strain of the virus began to spread. It had started late the year before in Étaples, in northern France; modern epidemiologists believe a strain of avian flu mutated to infect pigs kept near the front line for army rations, then mutated again and made the jump to humans in a huge transit camp near the town. There was also a field hospital there and the virus quickly reached it, either through direct transmission, or when men who'd passed through the camp reached the front, became seriously ill and were evacuated back to the hospital. From Étaples the disease was brought back to England in the bodies of sick soldiers; horrifyingly, the medical evacuation system, the most efficient ever devised up to that time, seems to have unwittingly acted as a highway network for the mutant strain of H1N1 flu. It reached Kansas by the end of January 1918, only days after it was first reported in England. By March, it was in New York. This first wave of infection resembled a more virulent form of normal flu; the young, old and weak were most at risk. A second wave erupted in August that turned the rules on their head; over the summer the virus had evolved yet again, and now it triggered its victims' immune systems into attacking their own bodies. This wave was far deadlier and hit healthy younger adults the hardest, but the first wave was quite lethal enough. By the time the second mutation began its swathe of destruction, up to 25 million people were already dead and, in early May, the disease had reached Highcliffe.

Rose Selfridge was 57 years old and in good health. Normally she would have shrugged off an attack of flu after a few days in bed drinking lemon tea and chicken soup, but this flu wasn't normal. Even the less terrifying first wave was a killer and Rose was just old enough to be in real danger. Sometime in the first week of May, the infection was brought into the convalescent camp, probably by a sick soldier or an ambulance driver, and Rose was exposed to it. The virus laid her low with terrifying speed, and before her body even had a chance to fight it off her weakened immune system was overwhelmed by a secondary infection: pneumonia. Before the introduction of antibiotics, pneumonia was a very serious condition with few treatment options available, and although there were army medical staff nearby, Rose's condition went downhill rapidly. She died on May 12, 1918, less than a week after first feeling ill.

Rose's body lay in state in the great hall of Highcliffe Castle, covered by a silk sheet on which Selfridge's employees had embroidered 3,000 red roses.[xxx] Her funeral service was held on May 16 in St. Mark's Church, Highcliffe, and she was buried in the cemetery there in a shaded plot under a row of ancient trees. Selfridge erected an elaborate headstone for her; a relief carved on it depicted an angel holding a plaque with her name.

With Rose gone, Violetta took over her work at the convalescent camp and Harry threw himself back into running the store. Within months of her death, Rosalie Jr. married Serge de Bolotoff, a Russian aristocrat. The family that had come to England in 1909 was broken and scattering, and Selfridge's own life started to tip slowly into a long decline. He had a long way to fall, though, and a few triumphs still to come.

CHAPTER 7: AFTER THE WAR

In his spare moments since opening the London store, Harry Selfridge had been working on a book. When he could motivate himself again after Rose's death, he published it. It was called *The Romance Of Commerce* and it was a history of retailing through the ages. He also moved forward with his plans for Hengistbury Head, purchasing the land in 1919. His plan was to build an enormous castle there, with 250 bedrooms, a private theater and a surrounding wall four miles long. For the first time, though, he was making a plan that he would never carry through. The work of designing the castle progressed in fits and starts but building work never began.

Tragedy struck again in 1924 when his mother Lois, his constant companion for his entire life, died suddenly. She was buried beside Rose in the Highcliffe churchyard, and once again he set about going on with his life. Enough time had passed since Rose's death for him to re-enter the social scene and he embarked on a new series of relationships. Among the women he was linked to over the next few years were the Dolly Sisters, identical twins who had achieved some fame as dancers and actresses. A string of other showgirls followed, and he lavished money and gifts on all of them. He was also indulging his love of gambling, but unfortunately, his enthusiasm outpaced his luck and he lost a steady stream of money. He lost £5,000 at casinos in 1921, when the average wage in Britain was around £500 a year.[xxxi] It didn't help that the Dolly Sisters were also gambling addicts; the three of them would visit casinos and racetracks together, and they helped him gamble away up to £5 million. None of it mattered much, though; the store was as popular as ever, and in fact was expanding. In 1927, the second half of the building opened, doubling the retail area and adding the spectacular grand entrance on Oxford Street. As the building code was modernized, many of the internal partitions were torn down, making the sales floors even more spacious than before. Twenty years of advances in building technology meant the new areas were even more revolutionary than the original section, and the business went from strength to strength. Selfridge's personal fortune was slowly declining as money flowed out on horses and actresses, but as long as he was at the head of such a successful business, he was as financially secure as anyone could be.

Then, in 1929, it all went wrong. The stock market in the USA had been climbing steeply for several years; millions of people were getting wealthy as share prices continued on a seemingly endless upward trajectory. Prices can't rise forever, though. At some point they have to return to equilibrium, and in early September the first jitters hit the New York exchanges. After a few days, prices seemed to rally and business went on as before, but on October 29 – now known as Black Tuesday – the bottom fell out of the market. With the loss of investments, industrial production started to plummet; by 1932, output had fallen by 46 per cent in the USA, and 23 per cent in Britain – and unemployment rocketed. Suddenly people were spending less, threatening Selfridge's revenue stream, and Harry himself found that the volume of his investments had been slashed. Of course, he still wasn't poor, but for the first time in his life he was forced to retreat. He had given up the lease on Highcliffe in 1922, but now he had to sell Lansdowne House and move into a more modest home. Hengistbury Head was sold in 1930, finally ending his dreams of building a castle.

The Great Depression dragged on, with the low point coming in 1932. By then 3.5 million people in Britain were unemployed and profits in the retail sector, especially in the luxury end, were greatly reduced. Selfridge's was still making a profit but the board of directors were in a cautious mood, and they were rapidly losing patience with Harry's spendthrift ways. As the 1930s went on the economy slowly began to recover but Harry's personal fortune didn't. He was still spending money too fast, and was starting to run up considerable debts. His relations with the board grew increasingly heated as they repeatedly urged him to be more prudent. Their demands grew stronger after the Second World War began in September 1939, until finally they could take no more. Harry's debts had reached a quarter of a million pounds and the board, fearing that they would end up being liable for them, took the extraordinary step of forcing out the company's founder.[xxxii]

For Harry Selfridge, this was the end of the line as a businessman. He was 83 years old and deeply in debt. The board had awarded him a reasonable pension, but it was nowhere near enough to continue with the lifestyle he'd become accustomed to. From a multimillionaire with two luxury homes he was now reduced to a pensioner living in a rented apartment in Putney, a lower middle class area in southwest London. He shared the flat with his oldest daughter Rosalie but, for the first time in his life, his days were empty.

Cut loose from the store he'd founded and too old to contemplate starting again, Selfridge entered a steady decline. His hearing began to fail and his mind often wandered. He and Rosalie managed to get by on his pension, as he had all the clothes and other possessions he would ever need, but there was little left over for luxuries. Sometimes when he could spare a few pence, he would catch a bus to Oxford Street and gaze at the magnificent building he had created. Almost certainly he let his thoughts drift back to the heady days when his revolutionary new store had taken London's shoppers by storm. The store went on, of course, but he was no longer part of it. When General Eisenhower took over part of the basement as his headquarters, attracted by its bombproof concrete floors and the secure telex lines Harry had had installed, he knew nothing about it. The days when he could walk boldly in the great entrance and up to the chairman's office were long gone. Once, as he gazed sadly at his legacy, the police mistook him for a vagrant and arrested him.

Harry Gordon Selfridge died in his sleep on the night of May 8, 1947. He was 91 years old. His funeral was arranged on a low budget and his grave, in the Highcliffe churchyard close to his wife and mother, is marked only by a plain headstone paid for by his daughter Rosalie:

IN LOVING MEMORY

HARRY GORDON SELFRIDGE

1857-1947

CONCLUSION

Harry Selfridge's own life ended on a depressing note, with his wealth gone and his career brutally ended by the business he'd created. The Selfridge's brand lives on, though. There are now four stores in total, with two in Manchester and one in Birmingham, and the company has created several sub-brands to attract new types of customers. The flagship of the company, now owned by Canadian billionaire Galen Weston, is still the huge store on Oxford Street. On the outside, its imposing neoclassical façade seems timeless; inside, it's been remodeled time after time, keeping it up to date with the latest developments in marketing and customer service.

What would Harry Selfridge have thought of what his store has become? It's almost certain he would have been delighted. His retail career was marked by his willing-ness to innovate, to take risks and to go about things in a completely new way. Selfridge's, Oxford Street remains the store he created *because* it changes with the times; if it kept on doing things in the same old way, it wouldn't be the business he founded.

Like all of us, Selfridge had character flaws. His woman-izing and love of an expensive lifestyle were, ultimately, self-destructive. He made up for it by a genuine devotion to his family and an enthusiastic compulsion to give his customers an experience they'd never had before. He succeeded, too. We may take the shopping experience for granted, but we can only do that because Harry Selfridge created it for us.

[i] Fond du Lac County Local History Web, *D.P. Mapes' Account of Early Ripon, 1870*
   http://www.wlhn.org/fond_du_lac/towns/ripon_mapes.htm
[ii] Wisconsin Historical Society, *The origin of the Republican Party*

http://content.wisconsinhistory.org/cdm/compoundobject/collectio
n/tp/id/46379/show/46363
[iii] Selfridges.com, *Images*
   http://images.selfridges.com/is/image/selfridges/herit-timeline-
01?scl=1
[iv] Woodhead, Lindy (2013), *Shopping, Seduction & Mr Selfridge*
[v] Milwaukee Journal, Sep 7, 1932, *The Yankee Who Taught Brit-
ishers That "The Customer Is Always Right"*
http://www.wisconsinhistory.org/wlhba/articleView.asp?pg=1&or
derby=&id=11176&pn=1&key=selfridge&cy=
[vi] Milwaukee Journal, Sep 7, 1932, *The Yankee Who Taught Brit-
ishers That "The Customer Is Always Right"*
http://www.wisconsinhistory.org/wlhba/articleView.asp?pg=1&or
derby=&id=11176&pn=1&key=selfridge&cy=
[vii] Justia, *Laidlaw v. Organ – 15 U.S. 178 (1817)*
   http://supreme.justia.com/cases/federal/us/15/178/case.html
[viii] Not Always Right, *Funny & Stupid Customer Stories*
   http://notalwaysright.com/
[ix] US Census Bureau, *Facts: The Holiday Season*
   http://www.census.gov/Press-
Re-
lease/www/releases/archives/facts_for_features_special_editions/0
05870.html
[x] Brave New Talent, *Selfridges*
   http://www.bravenewtalent.com/selfridges
[xi] Comley, W.J. and Eggville, W.D. (1875), *Ohio: The Future
Great State*

http://archive.org/stream/ohiofuturegreats00coml#page/n3/mode/2
up
[xii] Buckingham, J. (1892), *The Ancestors of Ebenezer Buckingham*

http://archive.org/stream/ancestorsofebene00buck#page/n9/mode/2up

[xiii] Woodhead, Lindy (2013), *Shopping, Seduction & Mr Selfridge*

[xiv] Glessner House Museum Blog, *Harry Gordon Selfridge - The Chicago Years*
http://glessnerhouse.blogspot.de/2013/04/harry-gordon-selfridge-chicago-years.html

[xv] Lake Geneva News, Jan 8, 2004, *The Chatterbox*
http://www.lakegenevanews.net/Articles-i-2004-01-08-67545.112112_The_Chatterbox.html

[xvi] *Largest US cities by population – 1900*
http://www.biggestuscities.com/ny/1900

[xvii] Culture24, July 14, 2000, *Shopping in London, Roman Style*
http://www.culture24.org.uk/history-and-heritage/time/roman/20000714-07

[xviii] The Structural Engineer, 1943, *Obituary: Mr S. Bylander*
http://www.istructe.org/journal/volumes/volume-21-(published-in-1943)/issues/issue-11/articles/obituary-mr-s-bylander

[xix] Goodman, David C. (1999), *The European Cities And Technology Reader: Industrial to Post-Industrial City*

[xx] Goodman, David C. (1999), The European Cities And Technology Reader: Industrial to Post-Industrial City

[xxi] The Draper's Record, November 19, 1898, *The First Moving Staircase In England*

[xxii] The Royal Purveyors, *Selfridges: pioneers of Oxford Street*
http://www.theroyalpurveyors.com/fashion/selfridges/

[xxiii] Goodman, David C. (1999), *The European Cities And Technology Reader: Industrial to Post-Industrial City*

[xxiv] Woodhead, Lindy (2013), *Shopping, Seduction & Mr Selfridge*

[xxv] Selfridge's, Oxford Street celebrates 100 years, *Media update*
http://www.z-pr.com/pdf/09-03-11_selfridges.pdf

[xxvi] Spy Hollywood, *The Real Mrs Selfridge vs. The TV Mrs Selfridge*
http://spyhollywood.com/the-real-mrs-selfridge-verses-the-tv-mrs-selfridge/

[xxvii] The Bournemouth Echo, February 8, 2014, *Mr Selfridge's Castle*

http://m.bournemouthecho.co.uk/news/10991379.Mr_Selfridge_s_
Castle__When_Harry_Selfridge_came_to_Highcliffe_Castle/
[xxviii] Woodhead, Lindy (2013), *Shopping, Seduction & Mr Selfridge*
[xxix] Spy Hollywood, *The Real Mrs Selfridge vs. The TV Mrs Selfridge*
    http://spyhollywood.com/the-real-mrs-selfridge-verses-the-tv-mrs-selfridge/
[xxx] The Bournemouth Echo, February 8, 2014, *Mr Selfridge's Castle*
http://m.bournemouthecho.co.uk/news/10991379.Mr_Selfridge_s_
Castle__When_Harry_Selfridge_came_to_Highcliffe_Castle/
[xxxi] Tweedland, *Who Was The True Harry Gordon Selfridge?*
    http://tweedlandthegentlemansclub.blogspot.de/2014/03/who-was-true-harry-selfridge.html
[xxxii] The Bournemouth Echo, February 8, 2014, *Mr Selfridge's Castle*
http://m.bournemouthecho.co.uk/news/10991379.Mr_Selfridge_s_
Castle__When_Harry_Selfridge_came_to_Highcliffe_Castle/